Windows 10 in 10 Minutes

The Ultimate Quick Start Beginner Guide

(with Screen Shots)

2nd Edition

By: Bob Rye

Table of Contents

Introduction

Hi there, my name is Bob Rye and this is my book Windows 10 in 10 Minutes. I hope you find the 2nd Edition of this quick start user guide helpful.

Windows 10 is the ultimate operating system experience. Microsoft put together the best features of the latest operating systems (7, 8, and 8.1), and added new apps and options. Additionally, Microsoft developed a platform that keeps all personal devices linked and synchronized with the new technological development. Although it is not the first platform to feature the option to purchase apps and run them on different devices, the Universal Windows Platform is the first to offer true innovation.

The operating system is the soul of any device. Although good hardware gives the user the capability to run different operations, only by being comfortable with its operating system will users find the real value of their investment and maximize their overall experience with the device.

Now that you have decided to purchase a device with Windows 10 operating system, or to upgrade from windows 7, 8 or 8.1, we are pleased to fill you in on all the basics to enhance your experience. But remember, you will also need to keep checking for updates to learn new features as they are added, since Windows continues development even after the official releases of all their operating systems.

System Requirements

Microsoft designed Windows 10 to be accessible for the greatest percentage of users. Most of the users that already have the most recent versions of Windows (7, 8, and 8.1) will be able to upgrade to the new operating system without making major changes to their hardware. This is one of the strongest advantages of upgrading, because most of the users will experience a substantial enhancement in the performance of their previous apps as well as the number of frames per second in some video players and games.

Minimum System Requirements

Processor:

1 GHz and above processor required

Hard Disk Space:

16 GB for 32-bit Windows OS or 20 GB for 64-bit Windows OS

RAM:

1 GB (Gigabyte) for 32 bit Windows OS or 2 GB (Gigabyte) for 64 bit Windows OS

Graphics Card:

Direct X9 and higher having Windows Display Driver Module 1.0 Driver

Resolution / Display

800x600 Resolution

Important Details

- When installing Windows 10 onto a device, you must ascertain that there is enough hard disk space, or the set up process will require additional resources. This is especially important for devices with 32 GB of hard disk space; in these cases, the set up interface might ask you to insert a USB flash device, SD, or Micro SD card with additional storage to complete the installation.

- Some older devices might appear to have inadequate space after upgrading, but you always have the option of deleting the temporary files and the backup archives of the previous operating system to regain a part of the previous space.

- The Cortana feature needs a high fidelity microphone to obtain the best possible benefit from the software.

- The Windows Hello feature requires a special infrared camera or a fingerprint reader that supports the biometric reader framework.

- To use the touch features, you will need a tablet or a multi-touch screen.

- A Microsoft account is required for some features to be launched.

- Some games and programs require DirectX 10 or higher for better performance.

Free Upgrade Requirements

Windows 10 has been available since July 29, 2015. The upgrade will be free for the first year for all qualified users, which implies running your current Windows 7, 8 or 8.1 operating system with the proper activation (Legal License) and some updates. This means that most current users will be able to pre-order their free upgrade during the current year.

- The updates won't be a problem if you have activated the automatic update system; you probably already met this requirement without even noticing.

- If you are license qualified, look in the lower right corner of the screen and you will probably see a new icon. If you put the cursor over it, there should be a pop-up message saying "Get Windows 10"

- Clicking on that icon will send you directly to the webpage where Microsoft explains in detail how to acquire the free upgrade and how it works. Keep in mind that the pre-order option to place your upgrade request will be placed in line, so it could take some time. You will likely find that it has been approved without notice. Windows 10 will be automatically downloaded to your device when it's available, and then the interface will let you choose the right moment to proceed with the installation.

- Windows 10 is service-oriented, which means that you will have the full upgrade on your device, not just a free-trial or shareware version of the Operating System. Microsoft posted that Windows 10 will be a full upgrade to freely run through the lifetime of your device.

- If you have a non-legit version of Windows 7, 8, or 8.1, you should legalize the Operating System; it will still cost you less than waiting an entire year until Windows 10 is available for purchase at approximately $199.

- You can also get a clean installation of Windows 10 after the upgrade, in order to improve the performance of your device and adapting it to the new features:

  1st Step: Click on Windows 10 Start Menu and then on Settings.

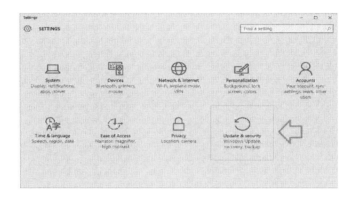

2nd Step: Click on Update & Security interface.

3rd Step: Once in there click on Reset This PC (Make sure you have backed up the important information you need on the cloud or an external device).

- If you don't want to wait for the upgrading request approval, there is another option to upgrade your current version of Windows 7, 8 or 8.1. You may create a Media Device (DVD) or a USB Flash Drive, because it can work on a device without optical drive. 1st Step: Acquire the *Media Creation Tool from Microsoft;* you will need to choose between 32-bit and 64-bit options to ensure that you are getting the version that will work better on your device, depending on your processor architecture. 2nd Step: Start the *Media Creation Tool* and choose *Create Installation Media for Another PC* and then click next. 3rd Step: Customize your installation device details (Language[1], edition[2] and architecture[3]) and click on Next. 4th Step: Choose between *media device* and *USB Flash Drive;* wait for the internet connection to download the archives. 5th Step: Insert your chosen *media device or USB flash drive* in the computer running Windows 7, 8, or 8.1 version. Start the set up application and choose which files you want to keep on the device, then wait until the installation process ends and enjoy! (If you want to install Windows 10 on a completely new computer,

---

[1] Arabic, Bulgarian, Chinese (Traditional), Chinese (Simplified), Chinese (Hong Kong), Croatian, Czech, Danish, Dutch, English (US), English (UK), Estonian, Finnish, French, German, Greek, Hebrew, Hungarian, Italian, Japanese, Korean, Latvian, Lithuanian, Norwegian, Bokmal, Polish, Portuguese (Brazil), Portuguese (Portugal), Romanian, Russian, Serbian, Slovak, Slovenian, Spanish (Spain, International), Spanish (Mexico), Swedish, Thai, Turkish, Ukrainian. There are also additional languages to be downloaded in the different *Language Interface Packages.*

[2] Windows 10 Pro, Ultimate or Home.

[3] For 32-bit 3 GB are required for 64-bit 6 GB.

you will have to buy the license for Windows 10, so if your computer already has a license to install windows 7, 8, or 8.1 you will probably want to install that version first and then use the *Media Creation Tool.*)

- Install Windows 10 on your smartphone. It is a *Beta* version, but it is intended to help Microsoft in the process of resolving any problems and will give users the opportunity of testing the version that will eventually arrive on the market. At this point, the version is just a *preview* because the option to *dial a phone number* is not yet available; therefore, you might prefer to wait until the official release. The upgrade is limited to a list of compatible devices[4] that already run with Phone 8.1, but if you really want to give it a try, just sign up for the Windows Insider Program and download the app. The app's interface is user friendly and it will guide you through the upgrade process.

- How to install Windows 10 on a Mac. You must follow the same steps that we mentioned above and create a *media device* with the *Media Creation Tool,* avoiding the probable incompatibility that some Macs might show with the *USB Flash device.* Once you have the *ISO* file, copy it onto a USB and

---

[4] HTC One (M8) for Windows, Lumia 430, Lumia 435, Lumia 520, Lumia 521, Lumia 525, Lumia 526, Lumia 530, Lumia 532, Lumia 535, Lumia 540, Lumia 620, Lumia 625, Lumia 630, Lumia 635, Lumia 636, Lumia 638, Lumia 640, Lumia 640 XL, Lumia 720, Lumia 730, Lumia 735, Lumia 810, Lumia 820, Lumia 822, Lumia 830, Lumia 920, Lumia 925, Lumia 928, Lumia 930, Lumia 1020, Lumia 1322, Lumia 1520, Lumia Icon.

download it to your Mac's desktop. Keep the USB connected to your device during the installation process and have the password of the administrator account ready. Search in the Applications/Utilities folder and start the Boot Camp Assistant app; that basically will take you through the installation of a 30 day free-trial of Windows 10 (License should be acquired to continue using it after the 30 day period ends). The app will automatically turn your USB into an installation device. You have to create a partition to install Windows 10. After that, the system must reboot and you can start the set up interface directly from the USB. Choose the specified details about language, Keyboard settings, Time, and Currency formats. If you have purchased a license, then enter the Windows 10 Product Key. You must choose the *Bootcamp* partition to accomplish the installation and leave the rest of the partitions without modification.

Starting process and new features

Microsoft Account

Creating an account for Windows 10 management is essential, not only because you will have the storage info well protected, but you will also have simultaneous access to all your accounts with only one master key access. Creating the account is free and as we said, you will only login once to use OneDrive, Skype, Outlook, and other Microsoft services. And now, because it is the new way to simultaneously log in to all your devices running Windows 10, all your current personal settings will be automatically exported between the devices. This will help you to control documents and sensitive information on multiple sources, and without delay, giving you important tools for the strategic management of your time.

Start Menu

Windows 10 is the means of reconciling the advantages of the old Windows 7's Start menu with all the screen menu features that came with Windows 8 and 8.1. Users are no doubt pleased with this new hybrid that brings the best of both worlds to the new standard of performance that Windows 10 is capable of.

This menu also offers a few surprises for individual tastes; users can select from both concepts and configure the menu in a way that will work better for them. After installing Windows 10 on a PC or Laptop, click the Start button. When the Windows icon appears, the new hybrid Windows 10 Start menu/screen will be deployed on the left side of the screen. The column shows all the apps as they have appeared on previous releases. But now the column has expanded so that the right side displays a screen full of tools, apps, and other links, most, but not all, of them to Windows 10 pre-installed apps.

Just as in the previous classic starting menus, clicking on "all apps" will show you all the currently installed applications, both the default apps from the installation process and those manually installed by you. All it takes to access those apps is just a click of the mouse and you can begin to surf all the information on your device. On the right side you can also access all the applications by clicking on the name or the icon on the screen side of the column. The search field attached to the basic menu is one of the features that were taken from the old Windows versions, including Vista and now 7, 8, and 8.1.

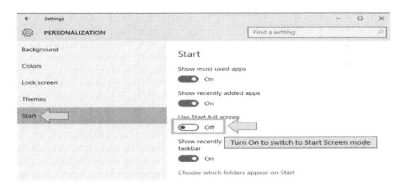

If you are searching for a special document or archive, you can type a command to see which are the current suggestions deployed by the pop-up tool, after the research. Remember that, in most cases, now internet links will be included in those results. The Shutdown, Sleep, and Restart options appear when you click on the Power icon in the lower left corner. This is a little different from the previous Windows 8 and 8.1, where users needed to log out before being able to shut down the machine. Some features on the latest version of Windows 10 were also implemented differently in previous versions of Windows 10. Now users can go directly to the "Account" area to change the picture, manage the sign out, or lock the account.

Unlike previous versions, the Start menu is now customizable and can be changed by right-clicking with your mouse. For example, when you want to attach a file or app to the tiles bar and make it instantly accessible, you will search for the desired app on the "all apps" section. If it is in the form of a shortcut in the desktop, you must right click it and then pin the desired icon to the Start. After doing that, the selected icon will appear on the Start menu. This option is also useful if you are looking to attach different applications to all parts of the interface so that you don't miss them. You can also attach icons to the task bar.

Say for example you need to manage some applications. Go to "All Apps" and click on the app you want to manage. Four options will appear: 1 Open, 2 Pin to Start Menu or Unpin from the Start Menu (if the application is already set up), 3 Uninstall. And the last one is 4 Pin to Taskbar or Unpin from the Taskbar (if application is already present in the Taskbar). You just have to choose the option that you want to perform.

If you need to manage tiles that appear on the right side of menu, first click on the tile you want to manage. You will see a menu pop up with three options: Pin to taskbar, Unpin from the Start Menu, and Resize. Almost all the apps will also have an option to Uninstall. If an application has the option of appearing as a live tile, you can choose from two options: Turn the Live Tile On, or Turn the Live Tile Off, which depends on the settings currently saved. So, you can simply click on that particular option.

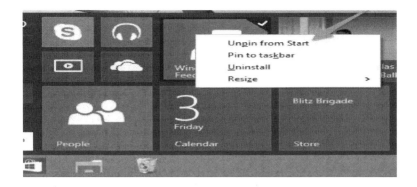

By customizing the left and right columns of the Start Menu, it is easy to control what you want to have in the Start menu and what you want to add to the tiled portion of the Start screen.

Many people felt that it took way too long for the Start menu to finally be restored. The main reason for this decision was the huge number of reviews from users asking for these features to come back; this is a good illustration of how Microsoft's focus is now on clients' service and satisfaction. Moreover, those who decided that Windows 8's Start screen was also cool still have the option to make it permanent.

Now let's take a look at the process for choosing the Start screen as the default system. Windows will determine by default which is the "better" option, depending on the type of device. If you are going to be working on a tablet or a cellphone (smartphone), then Windows 10 is going to choose the Start *screen* by default, and if you install Windows 10 on a PC or a laptop, the default option will be the Start *menu*. In both cases the default option will be enabled when logging in, but that does not mean that you cannot change to the option that you prefer.

Microsoft eliminated the Start menu with Windows 8 but, as we mentioned, most users were used to the user-friendly interface of the Start menu, and they were not pleased with the new interface. That modification opened a huge market for third party enterprises that started developing Start Menu replacement plug-ins and apps. However, the tablet and smartphone users and owners of the new multi-touch screen based PC and laptops were supposed to find the Start screen more comfortable.

In order to satisfy two types of clients, Microsoft decided to provide users with both options in the Microsoft 10 version. Without imposing one interface or the other as the only one available for each kind of device, Microsoft chose to let users opt for the one that better suits their expectations and needs.

Now let's see how you can change between the two options:

Imagine that you install Windows 10 on a Laptop or PC, and the Start menu is the default option after logging in:

- If you want to choose the Start screen, first click the Start button and then click the Settings command to enter that interface.
- Look for the personalization interface and click on it.
- Look for the option "Start" and then click to see the options.
- Look for the setting options on the left side of the screen, then turn on the "Use Start full screen." The button should now say "On" and be colored in.

- Now when you click the icon for the main Start button, the full Start screen should appear with the default icons and apps that you selected.
- If you change your mind and want to change from the Start screen to the Start menu, you just have to follow the same steps and do the opposite: Access the Settings interface by clicking on the Start menu and searching for "Personalization" And click on it.
- In the Personalization window, click the option Start to open another interface.
- The option "Use Start full screen" should be turned on. Just click to turn it off.
- After following these steps, the Start menu should be accessible as usual from the main Start icon in the lower left corner of the screen.

Every time you switch the Start interface option, it will remain unchanged, no matter if you shut down or restart your device. Whenever you want to change it back, you must do it manually.

Another option for choosing the Start menu or the Start screen

Let's assume that you want to use the hybrid Start menu/screen and your device has selected the Start menu by default. But what happens if you switch to Start screen and suddenly remember that there are some shortcuts that you need to use that are still on the Start menu?

- Follow all the previous steps to change your default start menu for the Start screen.
- Click on the Start icon and Windows 10 will take you directly to the Start screen. But at this point you

remember that there is still an icon that you did not put on the screen and need to access it. In the upper left corner you will find an icon composed of three horizontal lines, known as the "hamburger" icon; click on this icon. Now the left column of your Start Menu is also displayed on the screen, and you have the icon that you left behind. Now you have complete access to both Menu and Screen Start interfaces.

- You can now right click on the icon you want to put on the screen and select "pin to the Start screen," or simply drag it to the screen and it will automatically be attached and ready for use.
- At this point, you can click or tap the Start screen, and the Start menu column will disappear again, allowing your Start screen to remain as the default option.

Resize the Start menu

When you need to expand or reduce the size of the Start menu to accommodate the tiles you have selected, you can resize the Start menu at will:

- Make sure that your Start menu is enabled from the Personalization section on the Settings menu.
- Move the cursor to the upper edge of the Start menu.
- Drag the cursor up and down. You will notice that moving the cursor at this point will increase or decrease the size of the Start menu. By adding more space to the column, you can easily accommodate more tiles.

Width can also be changed by applying the same process to the Start menu, dragging the mouse outward from the right upper corner of the Start menu column.

Color the Start menu and Start screen

Now that you have the size that you want from your Start menu, or you have definitely decided to keep using the Start screen, let's see how you can change the color on any of these Start interface options.

- Click on the Start icon and go straight to the Settings menu.
- On the Settings menu, click on the Personalization link.
- One of the Personalization screen options (we will see all in detail later) is the "Colors" section. Now you can pick the color that you like the most for both the Start screen and the Start menu. Note that Windows can suggest a color that complements your wallpaper, but you can always choose a different one.
- You can choose to show the color on the Start, Action Center, and Task bar by scrolling down to the bottom of the pane and turning on the option.
- If you scroll up the pane, as we just mentioned, you have the option to let Windows 10 choose an accent color based on your desktop wallpaper background. If you turn on the option (by default it is off), Windows 10 scans the background and picks a color based on its color scheme.
- Now you can finally click on the Start menu and view the color, which Windows automatically selected.

Now let's see how to put a less solid color on your Start menu/screen if you want a smooth appearance on the device's interface.

- Go back to Settings, Personalize, and then the Colors section; scroll down to the bottom of the pane.
- Select the option that says "Make Start, taskbar and action center transparent." By default it should be off.
- Now access the Start icon and you should see a transparent quality on the Start screen/menu.

Choosing which objects are shown in the Start

Customizing your Start menu/screen goes further than simply pinning shortcuts to access directly. Let's see how this works:

- Return to the Settings interface and select Personalization, where we have been making all these minor changes. Now we are going to select the option for the "Start" menu.
- You will see a list of options; you can turn each of the settings on or off and select which objects you want to appear on the Start menu. The first setting lets you choose whether or not to allow Microsoft's suggestions about which content and apps should appear on the Start menu/screen. You also have options that let you choose whether you want "most used" and "recently added" apps, documents, and

folders to appear on the Start screen. You can also choose to have the Start menu open at full screen, and control whether jump list items should appear.

- You can now establish the apps and shortcuts which you want to appear on the list. To do this, click the link to "Choose which folders appear on Start" for easy access.
- On the customize screen, you should turn on all the folders that you want to see on the start interface.
- Now you can click on the back arrow at the top of the screen to return all the menus.
- Now when you click on the Start icon you now will be able to see all the chosen folders, documents, apps and other content that you selected for easy access on the Start menu/screen.

There is also another feature available through the Start icon; it is just a little trick that allows you to access some administrative settings and sections that otherwise would need to be accessed through various windows. This trick makes it much easier to access Power Options, Programs and Features, System, Event Viewer, Network Connections, Device Manager, Computer Management, Command Prompt, Disk Management, Task Manager, Command Prompt (Admin), File Explorer, Control Panel, Shut Down or Sign Out, Search, and Desktop. To reach this menu you just have to right click on the Start icon and it will pop up on the screen. The menu will be deployed with a set of administrative tools. This "hidden" menu is also available for all users of Windows 10 with multi-touch screen; you just have to tap and hold for a few seconds on the Start screen/menu icon and the same options will appear.

This makes it much easier to access many features for administrative management of processes, detailed and technical settings, and more. The menu helps you save time; for example, in previous versions of Windows, the steps to access the Event Viewer, System information, and disk and computer management tools may have required following a series of steps through different menus as in this example: **Start > All apps > Windows Administrative Tools**. Similarly, the Command Prompt, Control Panel, Task Manager, and Run commands may have been accessed only after accessing these menus: **Start > All apps > Windows System**. Now all these handy tools can be found with only one tap or click. In previous versions of Windows, right clicking this icon only deployed the taskbar, Settings menu, and the File Explorer.

Cortana

This is one bright feature that Microsoft has overhauled to work better on this Operating System. Making use of the microphone, the Windows 10 user will interact with a female voice assistant that helps guide users through a series of activities using the device. Cortana helps on web researches, basic numeric operations, and some other tasks such as finding archives and documents. The Cortana interface is user friendly and intended for a natural dialogue with the device, resolving some previous problems that similar systems had in earlier versions of Windows. The only drawback is that Cortana is available only in certain countries due to the language recognition packages that must be implemented in the Operating System to make it a fully functional tool. However, you can still use the feature if you consider that your speaking skill in one of the available languages is good enough to make yourself understandable to Cortana.

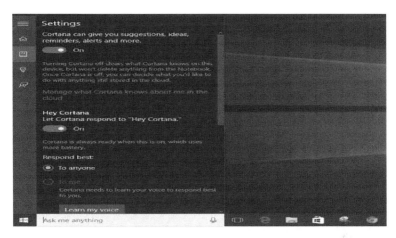

The digital assistant can be summoned by voice command: "Hey Cortana," but you have to activate the option first due to the fact that not all of the language packages have the Cortana feature fully available. (Windows 10 will include virtual assistants for all languages soon.) To activate, click on the search box located on the taskbar. After the menu is deployed, go through the steps to activate Cortana. Then turn on the option to let Cortana respond to your command. You can also manage which information is collected by Cortana to make suggestions, ideas, and reminders, and finally, you can set Cortana to respond best to you and learn to recognize only your voice (but beware if you catch a cold); otherwise, you can simply allow Cortana answer to anyone who gives a command. The correct method to take full advantage of Cortana's features is to say aloud "Hey Cortana" and immediately say your command. Cortana is always ready, and you can afford to use a little bit more battery to always give you a rapid response.

Multiple Windows Desktops

If you usually use just one monitor, or even in the case where your work requires more than one, having multiple virtual desktops is very useful. Windows implemented this feature quite some time ago, but now it is a full mainstream feature and not just some extra plug-in. In this final version of Windows 10, the option is fully functional and you can add a seemingly unlimited amount of virtual desktops to make it easier to manage different tasks. (Remember that Windows 10 runs all the apps right on the desktop.) Microsoft also developed a new Task View Panel; however, we are still expecting that new features will be added to make a fully customizable functionality out of this multi desktop option. You should cycle through all your currently open virtual desktops whenever you are changing between them so we strongly suggest you to categorize the apps per screen.

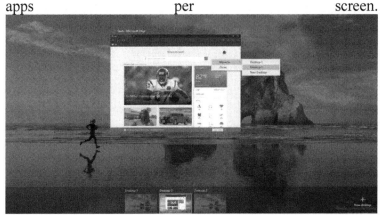

By default Windows 10 brings you three (3) fully functional desktops to manage info and open programs, giving you the possibility to simultaneously work several different processes at full size. Users can take advantage of the options given by multi-core processors in running multi-tasks by adding an unlimited amount of virtual desktops for shortcuts and other programs. You can drag a window and drop it into another desktop, and you can customize all your desktops; this is similar to the features that tablet users are used to having on their Android Operating Systems.

Snap Assist: Windows 10 has developed a more useful snapping tool to maximize the screens' options and help you work more efficiently. The Snapping feature was implemented in Windows 7; however, in Windows 10 you can work with quarters, which can help you a little bit more if you use a big screen. The snap assistant will help you in the process of organizing your screen efficiently and in less time. This feature, added to the Multiple Desktops option, creates a synergy that gives you more possibilities of working productively and full use of your multi-core processors' capabilities.

Edge: IE is no longer available with this Operating System, but Windows 10 has introduced a great innovation with this new Internet Browser. "Edge" is the new feature in the Windows 10 experience. The user interface is completely new, and the special feature that lets you ink, mark or write directly on any web page, proves to be one of the most innovative aspects in years. Now you can share your notes or save them with OneNote. This is a great advancement Microsoft's vision of what internet functionality should be. It has proven not only to be fun, but it also helps significantly in the search process and other tasks over the internet.

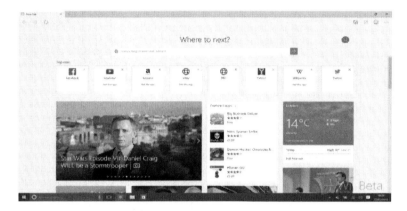

Settings Menu in Windows 10

Windows 10 version got rid of the Charms bar and put the Settings access directly on the hybrid Start menu/screen. Although not every control are there, a big part of the configuration options that your device has can be found there. This is the first step towards eliminating the control panel altogether, creating direct access to options:

> System: **The** user will find general settings to customize the features on their device, but technical settings will be accessed on the control panel.

o This is where you will find all the basic information about your device by selecting the last entrance, "about". First the device name is listed, the network (if already linked to one), product key and general information about the processor, RAM, architecture of the Operating System, and the option to link directly to the Cloud. Under this and all the labels of the Settings menu, you will find a list of related settings that let you directly access the control panel.

o You can manage the storage on your device on the "storage" option; there you will find all the information about hard disks, partitions, and external hard drives. This is also where you can choose the default folders for downloaded information to be placed when it has been directly downloaded from the internet.

o If you need to free some space or delete an application that is not being used often, then you have to go directly to "Apps & Features." There you will find a list of all the apps currently installed, ordered by amount of space or by name. The apps can also be ordered by modification date. If you click any user-installed application, you can move it to a different location, Drive, or Partition; additionally, you can uninstall it if needed.

o The system interface will give you the "tablet" option where you can change between tablet mode and PC mode; the option to sign up directly on one or both modes is also enabled in this section.

o "Notification & actions" is where you will be able to select which apps notifications are to be shown on the new notification bar, and the icons you have selected will appear there. This notifications icon is placed directly on the task bar in the right corner of the screen. It will be positioned across the right side of the screen. This is basically a new, better version of the Windows Phone 8.1 Action Center. This new notifications center consists of two parts: The quick actions at the lower side of the bar and the notifications area at the top. At the top you will find notifications of your social networks and the email account, as well as notifications from your phone number if available. You can select the apps from which you will receive notifications directly on the X that will appear when placing the mouse over the application icon. Or you can click "clear all" to dismiss all the notifications at once. In the "quick actions" section, you will have the ability to change directly between tablet and PC mode, a link to the display settings, and another to take you directly back to all settings. There is also an icon to configure your Wi-Fi options.

o The "Display" menu was reformed and seems more a hybrid of Windows 8 and 7 screens' resolution menu. Here you can change the screen size, enlarging icons, text and other items, adjust the orientation of the screen, and automatically control the brightness. However, to change your desktop wall paper you must go directly to the personalization menu.

o There is a limited list of options under the heading "Power & Sleep" to customize sleep options and the time before the screen automatically turns off when not in use, energy plans are not linked to this menu. To shuts down. To configure maximum performance or energy save, you will have to depend directly on the control panel. Remember to check the related setting on the bottom of the screen; you may find the options you are searching for.

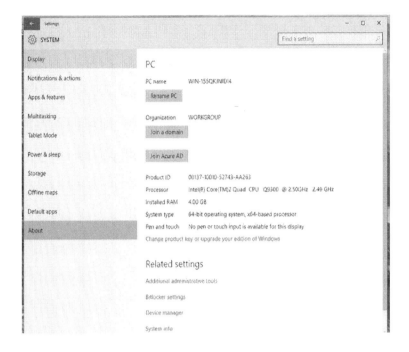

o Devices: This menu is to configure all the optical and accessory devices with basic options. It provides a set of useful options to complete the customization of your device.

o "Printers and Scanners": You will find the devices currently plugged into the device, as well as the program to print PDF and other documents. You will also find direct access to writing programs here. If you want to install a new printer or scanner, click on "Add Device" and follow the steps to make a clean installation of your new device.

o "Connected Devices": This is very similar to the previous one, but here you will find all the devices that are not listed above. There is a button to add new devices, as well, and you can access the properties of the devices listed. If your computer has a Bluetooth scanner, the device will automatically scan for all the devices within in its signal range, but in most cases you will have to install them manually.

o "Mouse & Touchpad": Here you can select your primary button depending on your writing hand, the sensitivity of the scroll function and mouse, and direct access to other mouse options directly on the control panel.

o "Typing": This option gives you the option to highlight or automatically correct the words while you are writing. It is useful if you are using the interface in a language different from your native-tongue.

o "Auto-Play": Manage your external media devices (Removable Drives, Memory Cards). You can choose to run media, open the folder, control manually.

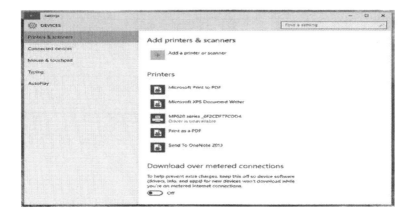

o Network and Internet: This can be accessed both from the Settings menu and directly from the Networks Sidebar. This section has direct access to the advanced settings interface.

o "Data Usage": This is where you can check on the amount of data used during the last thirty days. The sub-category of related setting is included on this panel so that you can these how much storage space is being used. This is useful when users have limited data plans.

o "VPN": This option is useful for people that want to create a private connection between computers. Users will also find cellular access and Wi-Fi options here, if they are available.

o "Proxy": You can choose to have proxy set up automatically, or you can do it manually by filling in the IP address and the current port of your proxy server. Using this configuration you can surf the internet while hiding your IP, or access content that some countries block. If you don't know much about this process, there are also plugins to automatically make those changes.

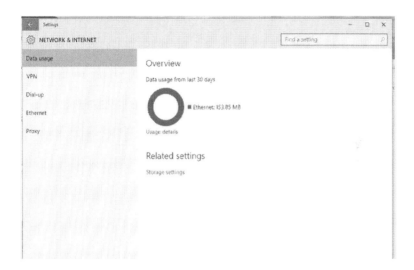

- Personalization: In this section you will find all the customization options to personalize your visual settings on the device:

o Background: the options here include, wallpaper, slideshows or images.

o Colors: you can choose accent colors for your opening screen here. Additionally, there is a link for high contrast settings to help users with special visual needs to find a color scheme that helps them. There are 48 featured color schemes from which any user can choose. Windows 10 also gives users the option to let the system automatically decide which color for the background fits better with the existing image.

o Lock Screen: In this section you can choose the design for your Lock Screen, which displays your choice of wall paper and the current date. This function is for locking the system when it detects long periods with no activity. You can also choose to attach some notification icons for the apps you want to monitor when Lock Screen is functioning, just like the options of the cellphone. Screen timeout is also located in this section, and also the option to implement a screen saver when Lock Screen is functioning.

o Themes: In this section, you can choose older themes to make your device gain a bit of performance speed or you can download new themes as they are released to personalize your device theme. You will also find detailed options to configure the Start menu/screen so that it suits your requirements. You can attach different apps, link different locations, archives, folders, documents, etc. so that they are shown in the desired order. Additionally, you can choose to start directly on the screen, which was a feature of Windows 8 and 8.1, or you can enter directly to the desktop and use the Start menu. You can choose and customize the option that fits better with your taste (This is likely a compromise for users that wanted the Windows 7 user-friendly Start menu, but it still gives Windows

8 and 8.1 users the option to continue using the new interface).

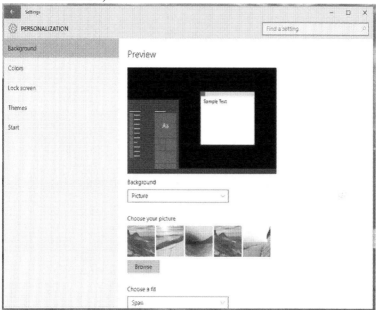

- The Accounts Tab: In this section you can find all the account settings to customize the access and other features of your account settings. The first option, "Your Account," is where the options of the primary sign-account can be managed; this account is always linked to Microsoft's Cloud Network. However, you don't need to be online in order to change your account's settings. Accessing this interface gives you the tools you need to make those modifications. Additionally in this section, you can change the picture you want to associate with your account, establish a picture password, and configure your PIN to start using Windows Hello. These tools help you to protect your device, giving you the option to sign in using a facial recognition technology (your device's camera must have it), the fingerprint or iris recognition.

- o The "Work access" option allows you to connect to a shared network with Azure AD.
- o "Family and other users" is the section where you can create additional accounts for others to access the device. This is an ingenious section because Windows 10 now differentiates between family and non-family members and gives them different options for access; additionally, it differentiates between children and adults. Now you can block websites that you don't want your children to access and establish time limits for general usage, apps, and games.
- o "Sync your settings" is the area where synchronization between devices can be configured at will. If you choose to turn the syncing feature on, you will have your official Microsoft network account information on your other Microsoft 10 devices. If you prefer to keep syncing turned off, it will be more like a non-specified account.

o Time and Language Tab: On previous versions of Windows, language and time were changed by directly accessing a small menu on the task bar. Now when you click on the clock you will be directed to the time and language tab. You have several different options here: set the hour and date manually, let Windows automatically change it, choose your time zone, and adjust for Daylight Savings Time. In this section you will also find the options to configure the language of your keyboard (default is English) as well as the whole interface language. In the Speech options, you will be able to configure the settings that let you use Cortana in your native tongue.

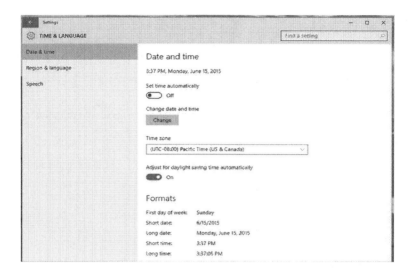

o Ease of Access Tab: Here you will find the options to make access easier if you have special needs. In most cases, these options will help you to use your device with minimum problems if you have some visual disability or related problem. Although Windows has always been recognized as having excellent accessibility options, the combination of Cortana with these options makes Windows 10 an even better Operating System for people who have some sort of physical problem but who still want to take advantage of new technologies.

o **"Narrator":** This is the option to make the device read aloud everything that is on the screen at the moment, including controls and text. You can choose if you want the device to read letter by letter, or by words. Additionally, you can choose the voice you want to hear, depending on the language packages you currently have on the device.

o **"Magnifier"**: With this option you can deploy a tool bar with which you can adjust the size options. This option is especially important for those who have visual problems and need to increase the size of the icons.

o **"High Contrast"**: Basically this is the section where you can manage the theme options to make it comfortable for sensitive eyes. This will help you to note certain parts of the text displayed, for example Hyperlinks, making them easier to read.

o **"Closed Captions"**: Here are all the options to configure the closed captions in the apps, Xbox videos, and other device apps. You can change the font, color, transparency, style, size, and effects of the subtitles. But these changes will not affect Netflix or other internet streams with their own pre-configured closed caption options.

o **"Keyboard & Mouse"**: These two sections do not differ from the Windows 8 version. You can configure the Sticky Keys and the Toggle Keys, as well as the cursor style. You can also change the size and color of the cursor, and there is an option to define when it's necessary to manage the mouse with the numeric pad.

- o **"Other options"**: The options included here are mostly visual options intended to make a pleasant experience with the interface; you can adjust these settings so that you will be comfortable when working with your Windows 10 configuration.

- o Privacy Tab: This section particularly has some options you won't find on the Control Panel, because this Settings Menu is adapted for all devices, including Tablets and Smartphones. This is part of the Windows intention to universalize the Operating System and make it easy to achieve a general comprehension of its usage. This helps users to comprehensively understand the OS functioning and performance, so that once you have it installed, it keeps all your devices easy to manage.

o **"General":** Here you can manage all the basic privacy options. Disable or enable apps to share information in marketing campaigns. Make Windows able to store information about the URLs that you visit in order to bring you advertising based on your behavior, store information about the language you use and deliver that information to Microsoft, focus on the webpages advertising on your key words, and enable Windows to show you tips for use, making most of the FAQ disappear through this sensible system. You can also view the privacy statement so that you may be familiar with the agreement you accept by using Windows 10. As you can see, this whole process of info recollection is focused on giving you the best options based upon your regular behavior.

o **"Location":** This will help most tablet and laptop users to change the availability of their exact location to the apps. Some users might find this very useful. For example, if you tend to order a cab through an app, you can clear all the info about your location, which is stored for about 24 hours by Windows. You can also select which applications are enabled to find this info available. The last link on the list will redirect you to the Microsoft's Location Awareness dedicated page for phone users.

o **"Camera":** Choose between turning your camera on and off, and also choose those apps that you expressly want to access your webcam. Usually the apps will ask you for permission before you start using the webcam. For example, during a video call, the apps usually shut down the camera after using it, but not always, which is the reason why you should check to make sure and avoid unwarranted permission to access the camera. This is important to restore the full privacy having your phone close to you.

o **"Microphone":** This is the same as the webcam options. You can turn it on and off and grant permissions for access, for example, when using Skype or Facebook. Note that the microphone should always be on if you want to use Cortana; otherwise, it won't work.

o **"Speech, inking, & typing":** This is a completely new section and is basically related to the way Windows 10 studies your internet behavior to bring you closer to your interests when using your device, and especially when surfing the web. Cortana is developed to understand general lines of behavior from all the information that it gathers from your speech, research, and typing. Activate it by clicking on "Get to know me." Windows will start collecting your speech, contacts, writing patterns, and your general research trends. Turning on this option enables you to search for anything and avoid typing. If you click "Stop get to know me" then you won't be able to take advantage of all the options that Cortana gives you to easily use your device without hands.

o **"Account Info"**: With this option you can manage which applications can access your account information; this is especially worth checking if you are using a single Microsoft Network Account and your info is being shared between all your synchronized devices.

o **"Contacts"**: Manage the access to all your social network contacts if those accounts are also linked to your primary Microsoft Network Account.

o **"Messaging"**: Enable or Disable the data recollection from your text messages.

o **"Radios"**: Manage the permission to Windows for collection information about the radio stations that you usually listen to. This is especially for smartphone users.

o **"Other devices"**: This option lets you manage sharing of information between your device and other wireless devices that don't usually synchronize with your PC, Laptop, Smartphone or tablet, such as your Xbox One.

o **"Feedback"**: This is an enhancement from previous versions; usually Windows asked you for feedback when troubleshooting and other difficulties. Now to continue with Windows 10's greater focus on service beyond basic problem resolution, Windows

10 has decided to interact more with its users, not only through the information recollected by Cortana's features, but also through direct interaction with its users. You can choose to send feedback to Microsoft once a day, once a week or other periods of time. Also you can choose how much information Windows will access about your device in particular.

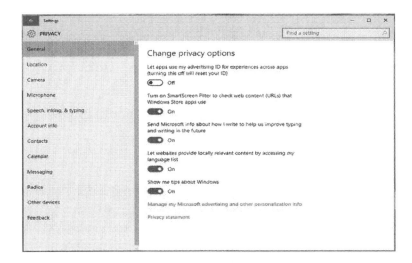

- Update & Security Tab: Windows update was completely removed from the control panel and now is only available on the Settings Menu; this is in accord with the new perspective of Windows 10 as a smooth experience. The Control Panel is minimized, leaving only the most technical customization. Searching for updates will now be available through the Settings menu, saving time and giving you the same previous options that were in the update section on the Control Panel, such as Windows activation, backup, recovery, Windows Defender, and developer options.

o **"Windows Update"**: This is the complete interface that you will be using to update most of the Windows 10 features. The automatic scanner will always inform you if the device is totally up to date or if there are available updates to be downloaded; it will also tell you if when you last checked for updates. You also have the option to manually search for the updates if you believe that issues with the internet connection might have interrupted the normal updating process. If you need to manage more options, you can access through **advanced settings.** The update history will be displayed there and you will also be able to choose how the updates are installed. In addition, this interface will give you details about whether certain updates have been installed or not, and the current status of downloads.

o **"Activation"**: Here you will find the information about the version of your Windows copy and if it is correctly activated. Additionally, you will have the option to change the key of the product, in case you are upgrading your current version.

o **"Backup"**: In this section you can configure all the backing up settings to generate your security copies. Backups created with the Windows 7 tools can be recovered and eventually restored through this option.

o **"Recovery"**: These are the basic tools provided by Windows 10 to help you resolve your computer problems. "Reset this PC" will help you do a complete clean installation of Windows 10 where you can choose to delete all files or keep those you find important. "Go back to an earlier build" will help you install a previous version of Windows 10; eventually this option will be limited to uninstall updates. The "advanced start up" is a powerful tool that lets you restart the computer by accessing through a different device and also configure external start up devices in order to help you install Windows 10 on different computers or simply keep a safe original copy in case troubleshooting makes re-installation necessary.

o **"Windows Defender":** Provides you with a useful set of tools to monitor your device and keep network threats from damaging your data. By default all the information and archives are scanned in search of Trojans, viruses, and other dangerous objects that might harm your device. This is essential and the Windows 10 Defender can work in synergy with other tools for defending your device.

o **"For Developers":** This section is specially designed for programmers or other software developers that are interested in designing and creating apps to run in Windows 10 and other kinds of programs. Most users will not use these options; however, the invitation is open for all software developers to create new apps and help to improve the Microsoft's Windows 10 experience. These tools also help with the troubleshooting process for some programs, although this requires deep knowledge of the programming process.

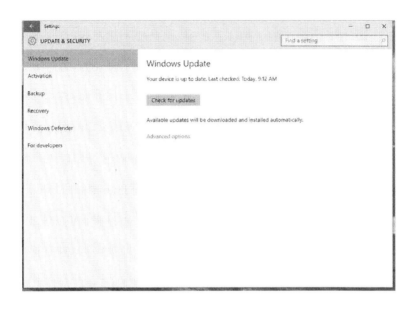

Some Interesting tricks for Windows 10

- Choose different wallpaper for each desktop: As we discussed before, Windows 10 has the option to open and create multiple virtual desktops even if you don't use multiple monitors, but we haven't discussed whether that also means that you can choose different wallpapers for each one of the created desktops. This can be done, in fact, and not by using any third party software. Is just that it has not been promoted as much as some other features.

  Here is the complete guide to set different wallpapers to each one of your desktops in Windows 10:

  1. Choose a folder to save all your different wall papers; it could be any folder, even any of the desktops.
  2. Hold down the **Ctrl** key and then select all the different wallpapers that you have in mind to use. You have to select wallpapers equal to the number of desktops that you currently have. Remember, there is no limit.
  3. Now after selecting all the images that you want to set as wallpapers, right click on one these and then choose **"Set as desktop background"** option.
  4. After following these steps you should see the different wallpapers on each monitor. There is also the option to cycle the selected wallpapers between the monitors; you just have to right click on the desktop and then choose **Next**

desktop background until you find the desired image for each monitor.

Note: Please make sure that if you don't see different pictures for each monitor, or if the pictures are constantly cycling at an alarming rate on each monitor, you might need to revise and change the wallpaper settings. If you think that this kind of configuration is needed, you should right click on the Start menu/screen icon and choose **Run**; after doing that you must access **control** **/name** **Microsoft.Personalization** **/page** **pageWallpaper** by typing the direction exactly as it is shown and click **OK**. Typing this command will give you Access to the **Desktop Background** window in the **Control Panel**, because it is not directly accessible through the main interface but still is available as directed. Now you should configure the details to make sure that the selected wallpaper is shown on each monitor. The desired options on **Picture Position** should be these: **Fill, Fit, Stretch,** or **Center**. If the marked options are set on **Tile or Span,** you won't be able to see but one image on the monitors. If you encounter a problem with frenetic cycling of the pictures on the monitor background, click **Clear all** at the top of the window. This will prevent all checked wallpaper from cycling on the monitor. You can also set separate pictures to all monitors as desired; simply find the picture that you want to set as wallpaper, right-click on it, and then select **Set for monitor** and the number of the monitor you want to place the image on.

- Stream Xbox One Games: Windows 10 now gives you the option to stream your Xbox One Games if the television is busy entertaining someone else. You just have to launch the app that is pre-installed with the Operating System, or it can be found by typing Xbox in the search engine from the start button. Then simply sign up with your current Xbox One account and click on the "Let's Play" button. Turn on your Xbox and check that it is connected to the same network as your PC or Laptop. Then make sure that game streaming is enabled right on settings. Select the Connect option on the left side of the screen, and then your Xbox should appear right on your PC screen. Now you can plug in the Xbox control on your device and begin playing right on the device's display. Depending on the router's speed, you can change the quality of the stream.

Apps

In order to connect to the Windows App Store, you need to have a Microsoft Account. It consists of an email id and a password which can be used for signing into Windows 10. You can use any email such as Gmail, Outlook.com, Hotmail, etc. As soon as the user signs in to Windows 10 using the Microsoft account, he gets access to all the apps in the App Store.

If a PC is used by more than one user, then each user must have a separate account. Each user can personalize their own apps, background color, account pic, and more.

How to check that you're connected using Microsoft account

1. Swipe from the right edge across the screen, and tap Settings, followed by tapping Change PC settings.
2. Tap Accounts, followed by tapping or clicking "Your account".

If you are already connected using Microsoft account, you will find your name as well as your email id at the top of your account pic.

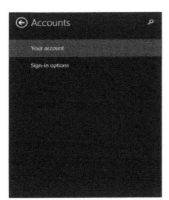 

If you are not connected using Microsoft account, you will find "Local Account" written below your name and a link to connect to Microsoft account.

Connecting your Account to App Store

Now since you have access to your PC with Microsoft account, you can easily connect to the App Store by just tapping or clicking "Store" at the Start screen on your PC.

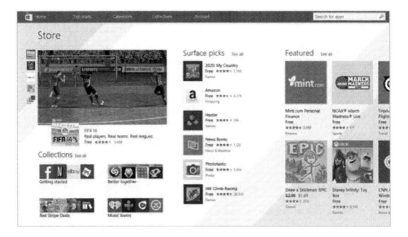

Finding and Installing Apps

Please keep in mind that before installing any App from Windows Store, you should have an active internet connection and sign in using your Microsoft Account.

If you are using a touch device, press or tap the Windows button at the bottom left of the taskbar.

Search for the Windows Store. It should have a shopping bag icon. When you click or tap on it, you will be directed to the App Store.

From the Windows Store, you can easily buy apps, music, movies and games. Since our focus is on apps in this section tap on the section "Apps". You can search for any app in the search textbox at the right corner of the screen. As an example, we will install the Flipboard app.

As soon as you find the app you are looking for, click or tap the Install button just below the description of the app. The button will be colored according to the theme you have installed, so it may be different than what you see in this illustration. You can use the reviews of the app and its pricing in order to be sure you should download the app or not. At the bottom of the page, you will see the platforms on which the app can run and all the languages it can support.

As soon as you tap the Install button, the app will start to download. Just check the progress bar to see the progress of the installation and wait. When it has been installed, you can tap or click on the Open button.

If you have turned off the Tablet mode, the app will work similar to how other normal apps run. But if you will turn the Tablet mode on, the app will cover the entire Window screen.

You can explore the different categories of Apps by tapping on the Categories section, as shown in the image below.

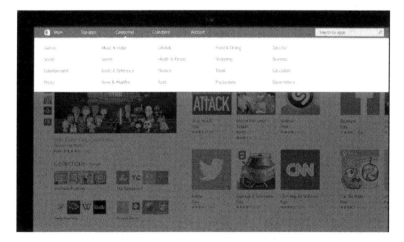

As soon as a new app has been installed, it automatically appears on the Start Menu.

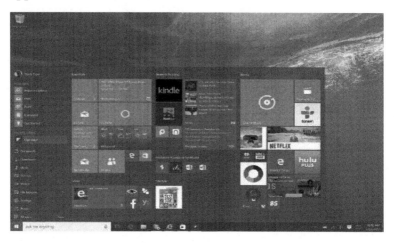

Managing Apps

Say for example you need to manage some applications. Go to All Apps and click on the app you want to manage, and four options will be there: Open, Pin to Start Menu or Unpin from the Start Menu (if application is set up already), Uninstall, and Pin to Taskbar or Unpin from the Taskbar (if application is present already in the Taskbar). You just have to choose the option which you want to perform.

Moving on to the next step, if, for example, you need to manage tiles which appear on the right side of the menu, click on the tile you want to manage. You will see a menu pop up with three options: Pin to taskbar, Unpin from the Start Menu, and Resize. Almost all the apps will also have an option for Uninstall. An application that has the option of appearing as a live tile has two options to choose from: Turn the Live Tile on or Turn the Live Tile off, which depends on the settings currently saved. So, you can simply click that particular option.

Now, suppose we want to manage the apps which are currently running. I have two applications open, the Photos App and Microsoft Word. In order to run a different application, I can simply open that application, and with the help of Taskbar, the switching of each application can be managed. But this can create a problem by causing multiple applications being triggered and clutter the screen.

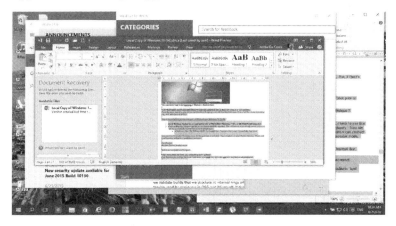

You can solve this problem of managing apps by creating another desktop with the help of task View. It is beneficial for users who have only one monitor display. Task View can be activated by clicking its icon in the Taskbar.

Closing Remarks

Windows 10 has already been downloaded by more than 14 million people all over the world. It has various new features for various types of customers, as described in the chart below. Look for your category, and give Windows 10 a try!

Should You Upgrade? *Windows 10 introduces a familiar experience that minimizes the learning curve for users upgrading from older versions. The new version also includes exciting features and enhancements that are fun, productive and efficient.*			
IF YOU ARE...	A HOME USER	A BUSINESS USER	A POWER USER
AND WANT TO USE WINDOWS 10 FOR...	ENTERTAINMENT	CONNECTIVITY/SECURITY	EFFICIENCY/RELIABILITY
UPGRADE AND TAKE ADVANTAGE OF...	• Improved modern Entertainment apps. • DirectX 12 improved Gaming Graphics • Microsoft Edge • Cortana Digital Assistant • XBOX App for Streaming of live games to a PC or Tablet • Windows Phone Companion	• Windows Update for Business • Windows Hello & Passport • Device Guard • Office for Windows 10 • Modern apps • Microsoft Wi-Fi • Battery Saver • Cortana Digital Assistant • Familiar Windows 7 like experience	• Rollback • Peer to Peer Windows Update • Customizable Start menu • Task View • Snap Assist • Action Center • Customizable Universal Apps • Cortana Digital Assistant • Continuum

Printed in Great Britain
by Amazon